teacher's friend publications

Summer

a creative idea book
for the
elementary teacher

written and illustrated

by

Karen Sevaly

poems by

Margaret Bolz

Copyright © 1990
Teacher's Friend Publications, Inc.
All rights reserved.
Printed in the United States of America.
Published by Teacher's Friend Publications, Inc.
7407 Orangewood Drive, Riverside, CA 92504

ISBN 0-943263-17-4

THIS BOOK
IS DEDICATED
TO
TEACHERS AND CHILDREN
EVERYWHERE!

Table of Contents

Notes

Children are especially responsive to the various holidays and themes associated with the four seasons. Teacher's Friend has published the **"Summer"** Idea Book, to assist teachers in motivating students, with this in mind.

WHO USES THIS BOOK:

Preschool and elementary teachers along with Scout leaders, Sunday School teachers and parents all love the monthly and seasonal idea books.

Each idea or craft can easily be adapted to fit a wide range of grade levels. Kindergarteners can color and cut out the simple, bold patterns while older students love expanding these same patterns and crafts to a more complex format. Most of the ideas and activities are open-ended. Teachers may add their own curriculum appropriate for the grade level they teach. Young children may practice number, color or letter recognition while older students may like to drill multiplication facts or match homonyms.

WHAT YOU'LL FIND IN THIS BOOK:

Teachers and parents will find a variety of crafts, activities, bulletin board ideas and patterns that compliment the monthly holidays and seasonal themes. Children will be delighted with the booklet covers, bingo cards, name tags, mobiles, place cards, writing pages and gameboards. There is also a special section devoted to the sport of the season!

HOW TO USE THIS BOOK:

Every page of this book may be duplicated for individual classroom use. Some pages are meant to be used as duplicating masters or student worksheets. Most of the crafts and patterns may be copied onto construction paper or printed on index paper. Children can then make the crafts by cutting them out and coloring them with crayons or colored markers.

Many of the pages can be enlarged with an overhead or opaque projector. The patterns can then be used for door displays, bulletin boards or murals.

MOBILES:

Making mobiles are especially fun for all ages. Teachers may like to simplify mobile construction for younger children by using one of these ideas.

DRINKING STRAW MOBILE - Thread a piece of yarn through a plastic drinking straw and tie a mobile pattern to each end. Flatten a paper clip and bend it around the center of the straw for hanging. The mobile can easily be balanced by adjusting the yarn. (Older students can make their mobiles the same way but may wish to add additional levels by hanging other mobiles directly below the first.)

CLOTHES HANGER MOBILE - Mobiles can easily be made with a wire clothes hanger, as shown. Just tie each pattern piece to the hanger with thread, yarn or kite string.

YARN MOBILE - The most simple mobile is made by gluing the pattern pieces to a length of yarn, each piece spaced directly beneath the other. Tie a bow at the top and hang in a window or from the ceiling.

CLIP ART PAGES:

The illustrations on these pages may be used in classroom bulletins, newspapers, notes home or just to decorate your own worksheets. Cut the illustrations out and paste them to your originals before printing. The drawings may be enlarged or reduced on some copy machines. You are also free to enlarge the characters for other uses, such as; bulletin boards, calendar decorations, booklet covers and awards.

PLACE CARDS OR NAME TAGS:

If possible, laminate the finished name tags or place cards. Use a special dry transfer marker or dark crayon to write the names on the laminated surface. After the special day, simply wipe off the letters with a tissue for use at another time.

POETRY:

Children love clever poems. Use the poems in this book to inspire your students and at the same time record the improvement in their handwriting.

Each morning, copy one or two lines, or an entire poem, on the class chalkboard. Ask the children to copy it in their best handwriting. Have them write the date at the top of the page. The children can then collect the poems chronologically in a notebook. This is a great way to show parents how their child's handwriting has improved.

STAND-UP CHARACTERS:

All of the stand-up characters in this book can easily be made from construction or index paper. Children can add the color and cut them out. The characters can be used as table decorations, name cards or used in a puppet show. Several characters can also be joined at the hands.

The characters can also be enlarged on posterboard for a bulletin board display or reduced in size for use in a diorama or as finger puppets.

BULLETIN BOARDS:

Creating clever bulletin boards can be a fun experience for you and your students. Many of the bulletin board ideas in this book contain patterns that the students can make themselves. You simply need to cover the board with bright paper, (preferably only once a year) and display the appropriate heading. Students make their own pumpkins for a classroom pumpkin patch or creative writing apples for a Johnny Appleseed display.

Many of the illustrations in this book can also be enlarged and displayed on a bulletin board. Use an over-head or opaque projector to do your enlargements. When you enlarge a character, think BIG! Figures three, four or even five feet tall can make a dramatic display. Use colored butcher paper for large displays eliminating the need to add color with markers or crayons.

WHATEVER YOU DO....

Have fun using the ideas in this book. Be creative! Develop your own ideas and adapt the patterns and crafts to fit your own curriculum. By using your imagination, you will be encouraging your students to be more creative. A creative classroom is a fun classroom! One that promotes an enthusiasm for learning!

SUMMER

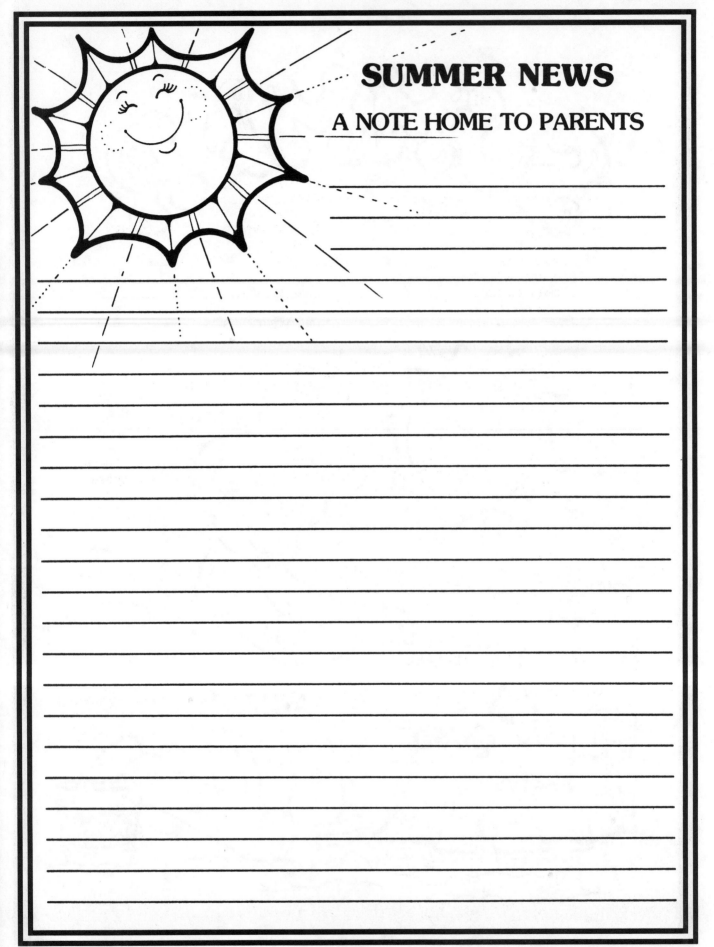

SUMMER NEWS

A NOTE HOME TO PARENTS

Summer Activities

SUMMERTIME

When every day is bright sunshine,
On a hammock, I'll recline.
A hammock strung between two trees
Rocked and tossed by gentle breeze.
Lying in the tree's cool shade
Sipping mother's lemonade.
Lemonade will hit the spot
In the summer when it's hot.
But, there are other things to do,
Swim and read to name a few.
Tennis, ping pong and croquet
are perfect for a summer's day.

SUMMER COLLECTIONS

Encourage students to collect simple souvenirs from the various places they visit during the summer. Examples might be; postcards, maps, placemats, brochures, etc. At the close of summer, children can make a collage of their collection and share it with the class as they give an oral report of their travels.

SUMMER MATH

Keep students up on math facts, even through the summer vacation, with this simple activity. Ask each student to bring in enough self-addressed, stamped envelopes for each week of the summer break. Once a week, during vacation, send one envelope to each child enclosing several practice math worksheets. Parents can become involved by checking the completed sheets. students will improve their math skills and at the same time have the enjoyable experience of receiving mail from their teacher, each week!

LEMONADE

A recipe for lemonade.
This is the way that it is made.

Measure one cup of each of these,
Sugar, water, juice you squeeze.

All of this you stir and mix.
Lemonade is fun to fix.

Add water now, one quart more,
Counting cups that would be four.

In hot weather, add to the mix,
Several ice cubes, five or six.

Summer Bingo

This game offers an exciting way to introduce students to the summer season. Give each child a copy of the bingo words listed below or write the words on the chalkboard. Ask students to write any 24 words on his or her bingo card. Use the same directions you might use for regular bingo.

SUMMER	PICNIC	FAMILY	CAMPING
SUN	BAR-BE-QUE	VACATION	HIKING
HOT	HOTDOGS	TRAVEL	COOK-OUT
SHADE	WATERMELON	PLANE	CRAFTS
SWIMMING	LEMONADE	TRAIN	BOATING
DIVING	ICE CREAM	BOAT	FISHING
POOL	4th OF JULY	AUTOMOBILE	LAKE
BATHING SUIT	FIREWORKS	POSTCARDS	RIVER
BEACH	PARADE	CAMERA	FATHER'S DAY
PARK	FLAG	PHOTOGRAPHS	GIFTS

SUMMER BINGO

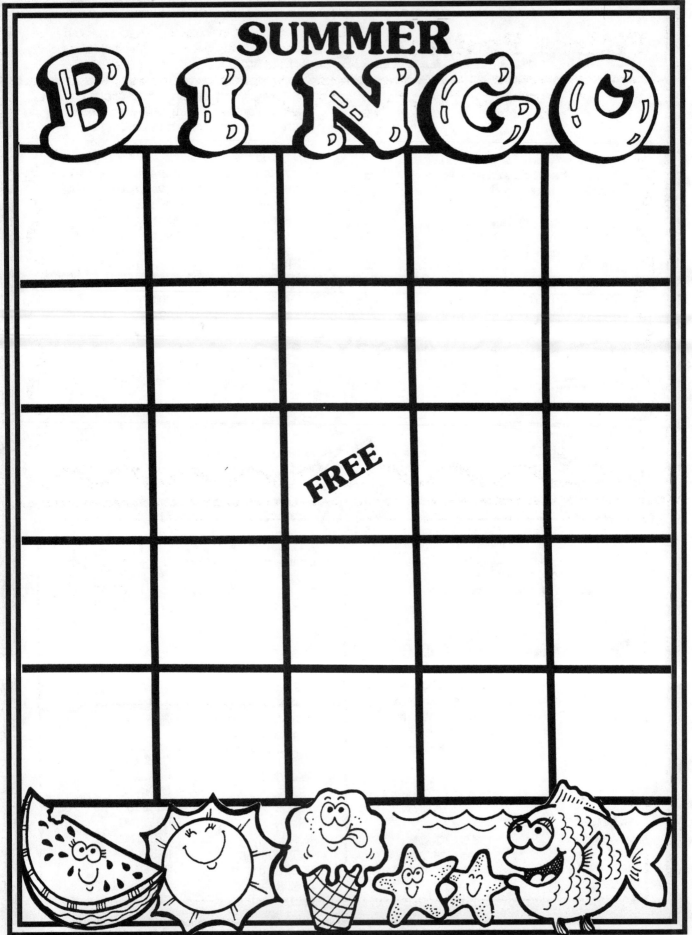

FREE

Picture Postcards

Copy the front and back of this postcard onto heavy paper. Draw your own vacation picture, write a note and mail it to a friend.

PLACE
STAMP
HERE

Summer Bulletin Boards

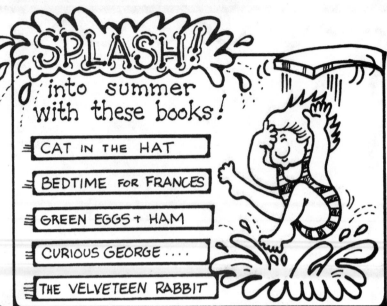

SPLASH INTO SUMMER!

Enlarge this cute swimming character on the class bulletin board to encourage summer reading.

List the titles of several books on strips of colored paper. Children might like to suggest their own favorite books and stories for the enjoyment of other students.

PICNIC GOODIES!

This picnic basket can be used in a variety of ways on the class bulletin board. Several baskets can be displayed, each with answers to math problems. The problems can be written on the picnic goodies. Students match the correct responses together.

The basket and goodies can also be used to display classroom monitors, reading groups, individual awards or vocabulary words.

SUMMER TRAVELS!

Roadway strips of black paper, with dotted white lines, can be pinned on the class board for a motivating summer display.

Children cut automobile booklets from construction paper and write their own summer travel plans inside. Students might like to be creative and write about fantasy travels, as well!

Display the autos on the roadways for a "moving" activity!

Splash Character

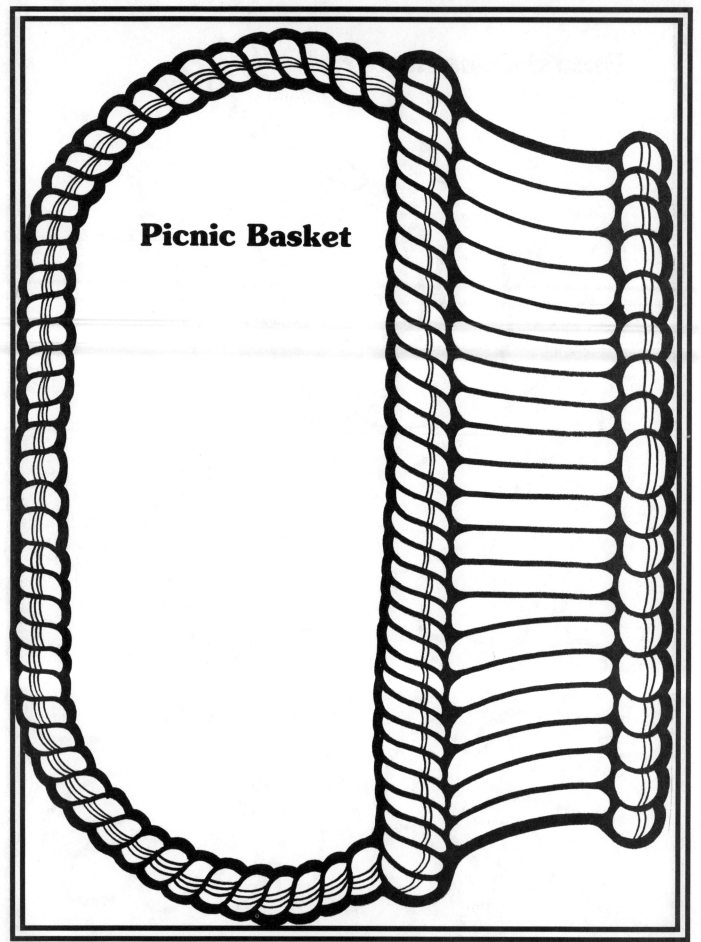

Picnic Basket

Picnic Goodies

Summer Travels

Suitcase Travels

Encourage your students to write imaginative stories about exotic travels using this suitcase booklet. The stories can be written on a piece of lined paper that is glued to the inside of the suitcase. Display the suitcases on the class bulletin board along with name tags that can be attached with colorful sections of yarn. Children will also enjoy decorating their own travel stickers, on the outside of the case.

SUITCASE RELAY

Your class may want to complete the exercise with this simple, but fun, suitcase relay race!

Bring two suitcases from home filled with a variety of old clothing. Each suitcase should have the same number of pieces inside. Divide the class into two teams. On the word, "Go!" the first player in each line, runs to their suitcase and puts on each item they find inside, (over their school clothes.) As soon as all of the clothing is put on, they must remove each article and place it back in the suitcase. The player then runs back to their team and the next player has a turn. The fastest team wins!

The team that finishes first, wins the game!

23

Sundial Pattern

Children will love making simple sundials and recording the sundial's accuracy.

Glue the circle sundial pattern to heavy cardboard. Cut the triangle from construction paper or heavy index paper. Attach the triangle piece to the circle by pasting the folded tabs in place, as shown.

At 12:00 noon, place your sundial outside on a flat secure surface. Place the dial so that the shadow made by the sun falls directly across the "NOON" mark. Now, on any sunny day, you can tell what time it is by where the shadow falls. Check your sundial often during the afternoon to see if it is accurate to your classroom clock.

This sundial will be fairly accurate for most middle latitudes. This would be a good time to explain to your students the difference between longitudes and latitudes. You can also explain how the tilt of the earth effects our seasonal changes and how this can also effect the accuracy of a sundial during various times of the year.

Fold the tabs in opposite directions and paste in place.

A   fold   B

NOON

Summer Mobile

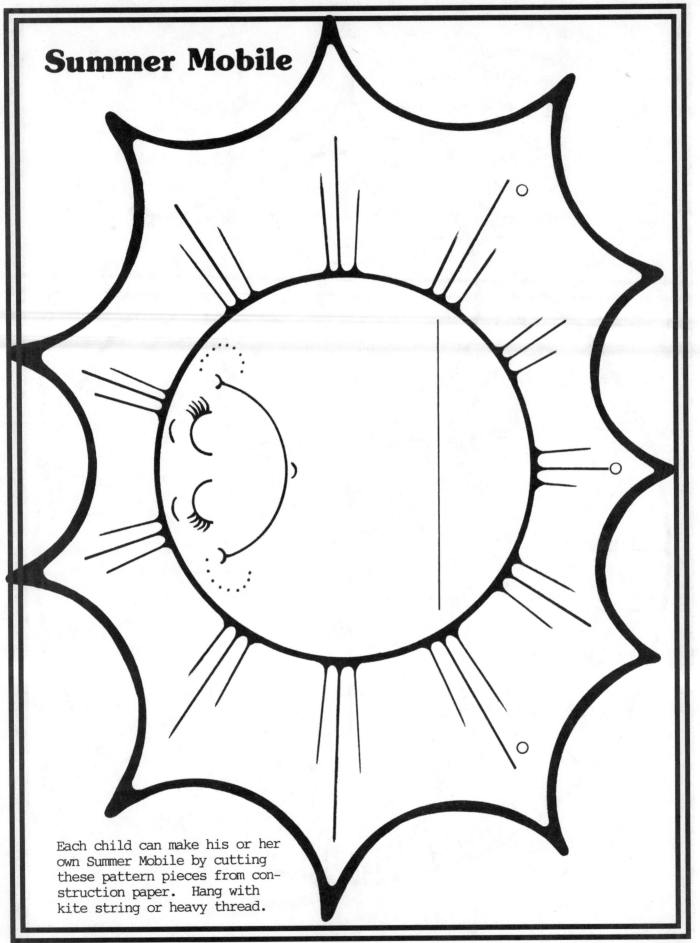

Each child can make his or her own Summer Mobile by cutting these pattern pieces from construction paper. Hang with kite string or heavy thread.

Summertime Characters

Make these cute characters from index paper. Color, cut out and fold. Bend the arms of both characters forward and staple the pail to the girl's hand.

Matching
Pail and Shovel

Make several copies of pails
and shovels from colored construction paper. Use them in
a variety of matching activities such as, letter recognition, math facts, opposites,
words and definitions and
so on.

JUNE ACTIVITIES	DEEP BLUE SEA MOBILE
JUNE AWARDS	STAND UP FISH
JUNE CLIP ART	FATHER'S DAY ACTIVITIES
JUNE BULLETIN BOARDS	STAND UP DAD
JUNE FUN GLASSES	FATHER'S DAY COUPON BOOKLET

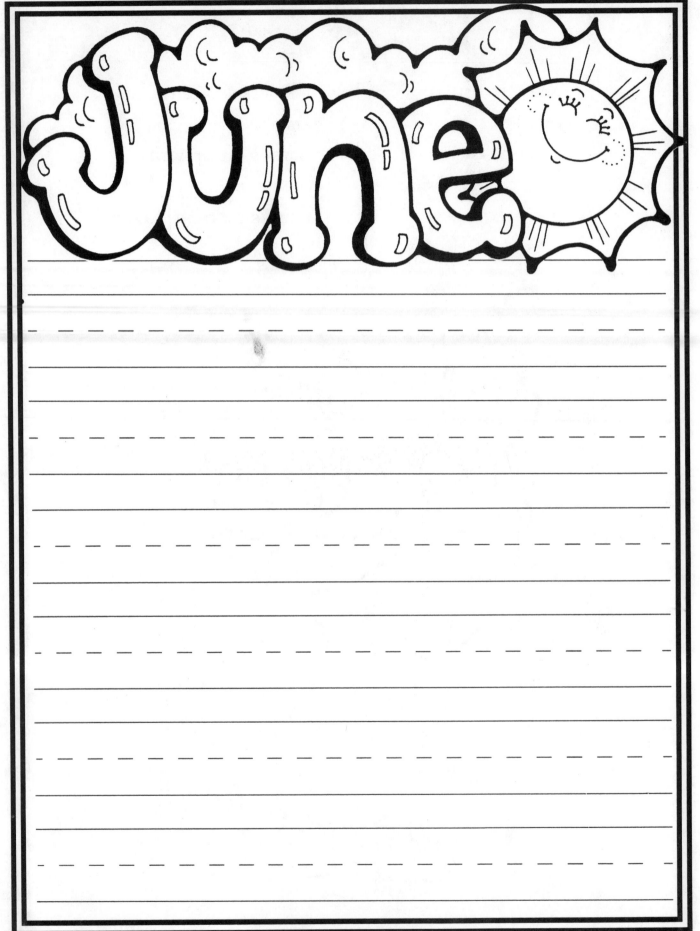

SUPER STUDENT AWARD

awarded to

_____

for

_____
_____

Date
_____

Teacher

STUDENT OF THE MONTH

AWARDED TO

_____
Name

_____

_____

Teacher   Date

Type the name of your school, address and telephone number in this space. Include your name and room number, also.

OUR JUNE NEWSLETTER

Suggestions for a June newsletter:

List the name of each student that was selected student of the week for the month of May.

Note the date of the last day of school, Flag Day and Father's Day. Make sure that parents know which days children will not be in attendance.

List the dates and times of award ceremonies and celebrations that will be taking place those last few days of school.

Tell about the special things your class has accomplished during the school year.

Staple the June cafeteria menu to each newsletter.

Ask one of your students to draw several small pictures about Father's Day or the end of school to be used in the June newsletter.

Ask your school principal to write a brief message that can be included with this year-end newsletter.

Thank all of the parent volunteers that have helped in the classroom during the year.

Announce any programs or special activities that children might like.

List various local summer activities that parents and children would find enjoyable.

Wish everyone a wonderful summer and make suggestions that might help parents reinforce good reading and study skills during the summer months.

June Clip Art

June Activities

THE MONTH OF JUNE

The month of June is quite unique,
with happy days in every week.
Good weather, weddings and vacations,
Flag Day, school's end, graduations.

Preceded by the month of May,
What's better than a bright June day?
The happy days will seem to fly
And then the month will be July.

What do you plan to do in June,
Marriage, wedding, honeymoon?
Diploma, graduation fun,
From college, high school or which one?

Display the flag, red, white and blue,
On the 14th, you should, will you?
The day in June I'm happy about
Will be the day that school is out!

YEAR-END SCRAPBOOK

A fun way to remember each member
of the class for years to come is
with a scrapbook!

Assign each student their very own
page to write you a note, include
a poem, a drawing or add a photo.
Make a cover from poster board
and secure the book together with
yarn or ribbon. Students will
love being included in this special
book!

WADING POOL READING

A small inflatable wading pool
can provide a novel attraction
for summer readers.

Place the empty pool in one cor-
ner of the classroom and encourage your students to use the
pool during silent reading time.

WELCOME NEXT YEAR'S CLASS!

This fun idea will give your students a chance to reflect on their many
accomplishments during the school year and at the same time welcome the
new class entering in September.

Ask each student to make his or her own "Welcome to Grade ___!" booklet,
from the pattern provided. Different pages in the booklet can be entitled,
"My Favorite School Project," "Favorite Books I've Read!" "My Favorite
School Holiday!" "My Tips for an Extra Good Year!" etc. The last page of
the booklet might contain a brief biography of the author. A photo or
self portrait might also be included.

When the new class enters on the first day of school, surprise them with
their own special "Welcome" booklet!

June Bulletin Boards

PLANS FOR THE FUTURE

Children will love making their own self portraits donned in graduation caps and gowns. Students can then write about their plans and dreams for the future on scrolls of white paper. Pin the portraits and the scrolls, as shown in the illustration, for a thought provoking and motivating display.

SUNNY AWARDS

This motivational bulletin board will certainly put loads of sunshine into any classroom!

Display a large paper sun and several triangle rays on the class board. On the back of each ray, write a specific classroom award, such as, "Extra 15 minutes at recess," or "Ice cream party on Friday!" When the entire class completes a required assignment, choose a student to turn over one of the rays to reveal the award!

DUNKIN' DOUGHNUTS

Children love doughnuts! Don't we all! Celebrate Doughnut Day on June 6th by having a class doughnut party. After the feast, children can use the doughnut booklet to write fantasy stories about doughnuts or creative recipes. Display them on the class bulletin board in this cute manner.

Doughnut Booklet

Name

My Plans for the Future!

June Fun Glasses

Cut the pattern pieces from heavy
index paper and color with markers
or crayons. Attach the bows to
the frame by fitting them into the
designated slots.

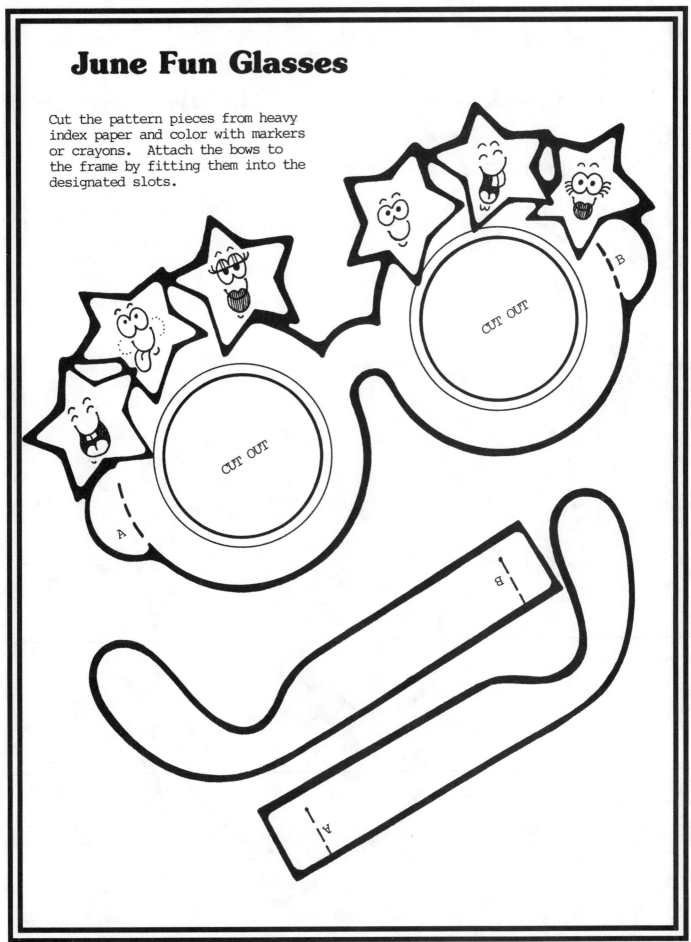

" Deep Blue Sea " Mobile

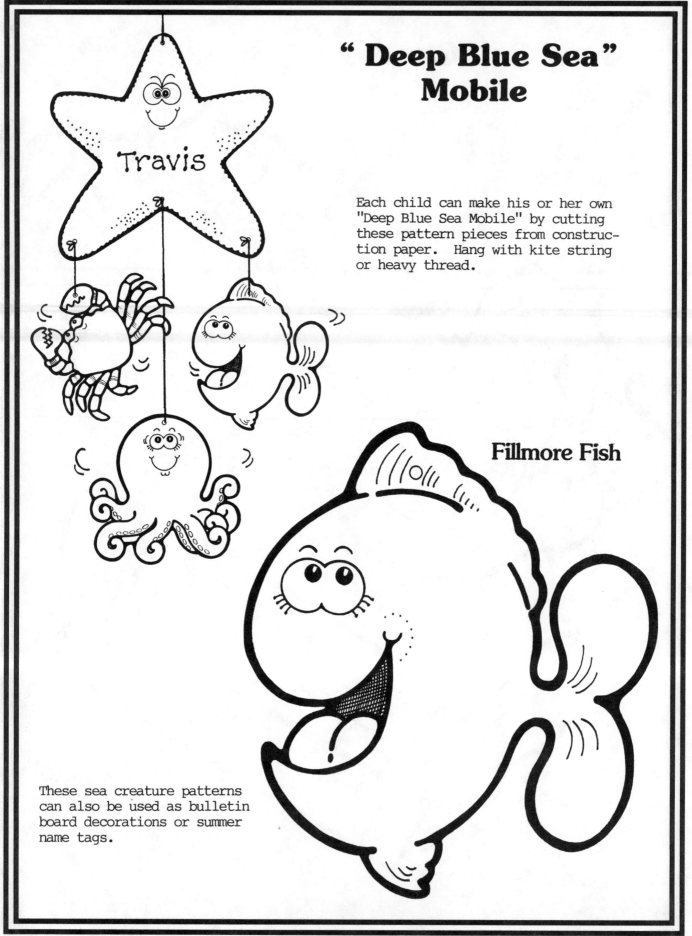

Each child can make his or her own "Deep Blue Sea Mobile" by cutting these pattern pieces from construction paper. Hang with kite string or heavy thread.

Fillmore Fish

These sea creature patterns can also be used as bulletin board decorations or summer name tags.

Stevie Starfish

Christine Crab

Oscar Octopus

Stand-Up Fish

Cut the fish and octopus from
heavy paper. Write your own
"fishy" message across the fish.
Fan fold along the dotted lines.
Glue the octopus to the first
fish and stand on a desk top
for a summer decoration.

Father's Day Activities

FATHER'S NAME

The children in Denmark
And in Mexico, too,
Call their father "Papa"
Like the French children do.

It may be old-fashioned
And a seldom used name
But in dozens of countries
Today, it's the same.

With respect and with reverence
This title remains
Nearly all the world over
Well known among names.

It's as well known as Father
And Daddy and Dad.
He's breadwinner, provider,
Good names he has had.

All over the earth
He's been known as Papa.
Revere him, endear him
And cheer him, Hurrah!

WONDERFUL DAD

Ask children to think of all the
things that make their fathers
wonderful. (Grandfathers, step-
fathers, uncles or neighbors can
always be substituted.) Have
them write their special thoughts
on colored paper and include them
in a Father's Day card.

STAR-SHAPED PAPER WEIGHTS

These easy Father's Day gifts are
a joy to make and fun to give.

Grease the inside of a small star-
shaped cookie cutter with petroleum
jelly. Place a cut-out photo of
one of the children in the center
of the cutter. Pour in a thick
mixture of plaster of paris. When
the plaster is dry, students can
remove the paper weight and paint
around the picture with yellow
tempera paint. Cover with a
coat of shellac for a glossy
finish.

RECIPE FOR DAD

Children will love creating "DAD"
recipes! Ask each child to write
a recipe using the ingredients that
make his or her dad special. Here
is an example:

In a large mixing bowl, combine
4 cups of security and 3 pounds
of love. Briskly stir together
with a tablespoon of generosity,
a dash of patience and a good
measure of discipline. Bake it
with the warmth of kindness and
serve it to all members of the
family. What is this special
treasure? My Dad!

Stand-Up Dad

Make this Stand-Up Dad character from index or construction paper. Color, cut and fold. Attach the "Happy Father's Day" sign to his hands.

Stand him on a table for a Father's Day decoration or give him as a card to your dad on his special day!

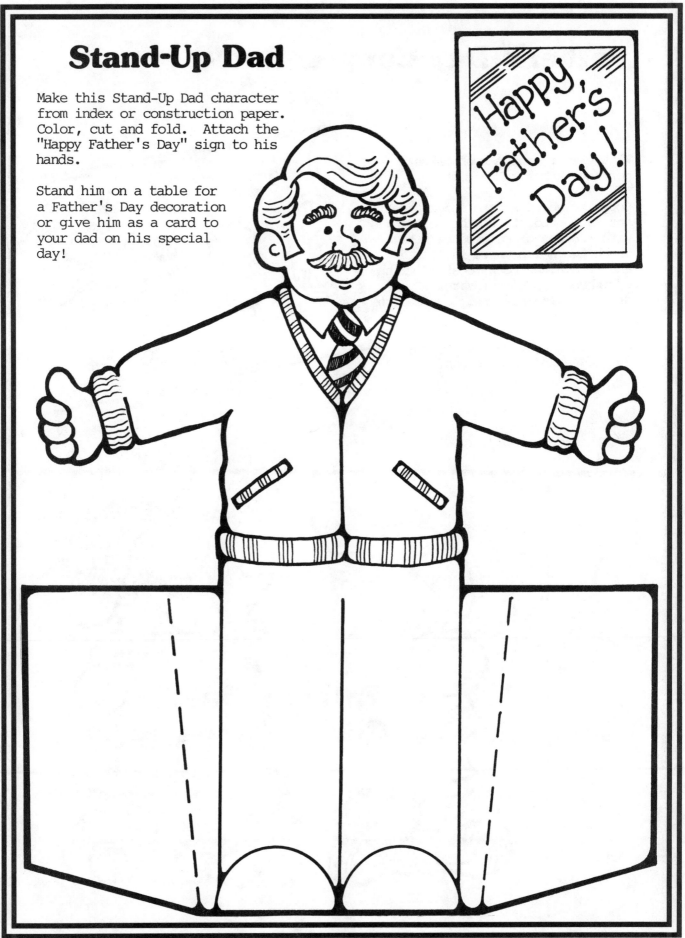

Father's Day Coupon Book

This clever coupon book makes a perfect Father's Day gift.

Copy the coupons onto index paper and have students do the coloring with crayons or colored markers. Punch two holes where indicated and attach the book together with a ribbon or piece of yarn. Children can also add their own coupons using the provided blank pages.

Dad will love receiving this gift and redeeming each coupon!

**Redeem this coupon
and I'll help clean
_____ !**

Father's Day
Coupon Book

**Redeem this coupon
and I'll feed our pets
____ times!**

Father's Day
Coupon Book

Redeem this coupon
and I'll help in the kitchen
___ times!

Father's Day
Coupon Book

Redeem this coupon
and I'll help
in the garden!

Father's Day
Coupon Book

**Father's Day
Coupon Book**

**Father's Day
Coupon Book**

JULY AWARDS

JULY ACTIVITIES

JULY FUN GLASSES

JULY CLIP ART

JULY BULLETIN BOARDS

ICE CREAM MONITORS

UNCLE SAM CHARACTER

STATUE OF LIBERTY

STATUE OF LIBERTY CROWN AND TORCH

UNCLE SAM BEARD AND HAT

STAND-UP SHUTTLE

MOVABLE ASTRONAUT

SUPER STUDENT AWARD

awarded to

_____

for

_____

_____

_____

_____
Date

_____
Teacher

STUDENT OF THE MONTH

AWARDED TO

_____
Name

_____

_____

_____   _____
Teacher   Date

July Activities

JULY

A flash of fireworks in the sky!
We celebrate Fourth of July
We celebrate this glorious day
In bright and beautiful display.
It's summer, every day is hot.
Cool drinks and shade we need a lot.
Hot dog and mustard on a bun
Is my idea of picnic fun.
Is there any food you've known
That's cooler than an ice-cream cone?

MY SUMMER DIARY

Encourage students to write this summer by asking them to keep summer diaries. Have them write about things they get to do and places they go. Ask them to also write about events and activities they wish could have happened. They may want to include special jokes or riddles or even summer movie reviews.

STUDENT-MADE ICE CREAM

Children will love making their own ice cream in the classroom! Here's an easy recipe that doesn't require an old-fashioned ice cream maker. The only equipment needed is an electric mixer, three bowls, ice cube trays without dividers and use of the freezer space of any refirgerator.

For every 12 servings you will need:

2 cups of milk	1 tablespoon of vanilla
4 eggs	2 cups of whipping cream
1 cup of honey	2 ripe bananas

Beat the eggs in a large bowl adding the milk slowly. Continue to beat as you add the honey and vanilla. Mash the banana and add to the mixture. In a separate bowl, beat the whipping cream until it forms soft peaks. Fold the whipped cream into the egg and banana mixture. Pour into ice cube trays and partially freeze, (about 2 hours.) Return the frozen mixture to a large bowl and beat once again with the mixer. Serve, right away, in small paper cups and enjoy!

(If your ice cream becomes too slushy, simply place it back into the freezer for a few minutes before serving.)

Type the name of your school,
address and telephone number
in this space. Include your
name and room number, also.

Suggestions for a July newsletter:

 If your school is still in session, list the name of each student that was selected student of the week for the month of June.

Note the dates of Independence Day. Make sure that parents know which days children will not be in attendance.

Announce special programs being conducted by your school or in your classroom.

Ask one of your students to draw several small pictures about summer and the 4th of July to be used in the July newsletter.

 If your school is not in session during the summer months, you might like to mail a newsletter home to parents. This will require more time and organization, but it could be a real boost to each child's education at home.

Include some math activities or worksheets with the newsletter. A reading list might also be included.

List several safety precautions that should be observed during the summer months.

Tell the parents and students about your vacation plans.

Encourage parents to take their child to the public library or local museum.

Include a summer calendar noting creative activites that children might do each day of the vacation.

July Fun Sunglasses

Cut the pattern pieces from heavy index paper and color with markers or crayons.

Attach the bows to the frame by fitting them into the designated slots.

July Clip Art

July Bulletin Boards

GET THE SCOOP!

This huge ice cream sundae provides a "delicious" way to encourage classroom participation.

Represent each child with a big paper scoop of ice cream on the class board. Students can add glitter "candy sprinkles," cotton "Whip cream" and red paper "cherries" to the class sundae when particular accomplishments are reached.

COOL RULES!

This extra large, multi-decked, ice cream cone offers an excellent way to remind students of classroom rules or procedures.

Encourage the appropriate behavior by labeling the display, "Cool Rules." Schedule a class ice cream party as students' behavior improves.

REACH FOR THE STARS!

Create a space theme in your classroom with this easy idea.

Display a large rocketship on the board along with several movable astronauts. Sections of yarn, (lifelines) can be attached to each astronaut.

Children can decorate the background with drawings of stars and planets.

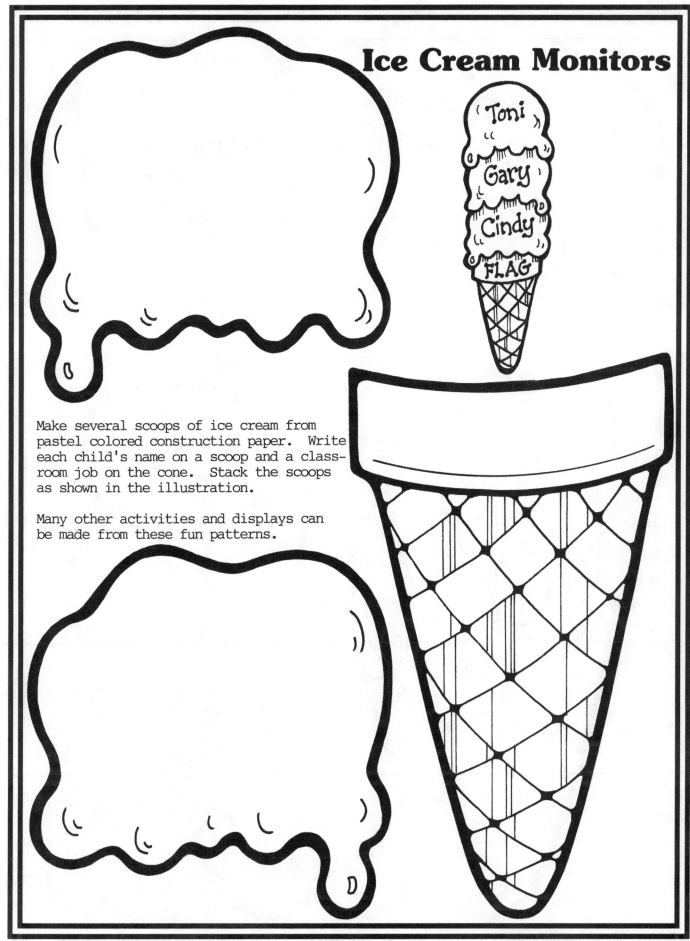

Make several scoops of ice cream from pastel colored construction paper. Write each child's name on a scoop and a classroom job on the cone. Stack the scoops as shown in the illustration.

Many other activities and displays can be made from these fun patterns.

MY ICE CREAM BOOK

The Flag of the United States of America

Uncle Sam Character

Make this cute Uncle Sam Character from index paper. Color, cut out and fold. Attach the flag to his right hand.

Use him as a table decoration for the 4th of July!

Statue of Liberty

This cute Statue of Liberty is made from heavy index paper. Color, cut out and fold to make her stand on a table. Secure the torch to her right hand.

Statue of Liberty Crown

Children will love making this simple Statue of Liberty Crown!

Cut the center from a paper plate, as shown, and fold back each end. Cut five points from construction paper and staple or glue in place. Color with crayons, paints or sprinkle with glitter.

This crown should easily set on a child's head without the aid of hairpins.

Liberty Torch Pattern

Color the torch patterns and cut them from heavy paper. Assemble them as shown. Use a cardboard tube, from a used roll of paper towels, for the handle of the torch.

1. Place the tube or handle of the torch through the center hole of the pattern. Fold the edges upward to form the base of the torch.

2. Fold the bottom of the flame in opposite directions and place in the tube. You may wish to tape or glue it in place.

1.

2.

CUT

CUT

CUT

CUT

CUT

CUT

CUT OUT

CUT

CUT

Uncle Sam Beard Pattern

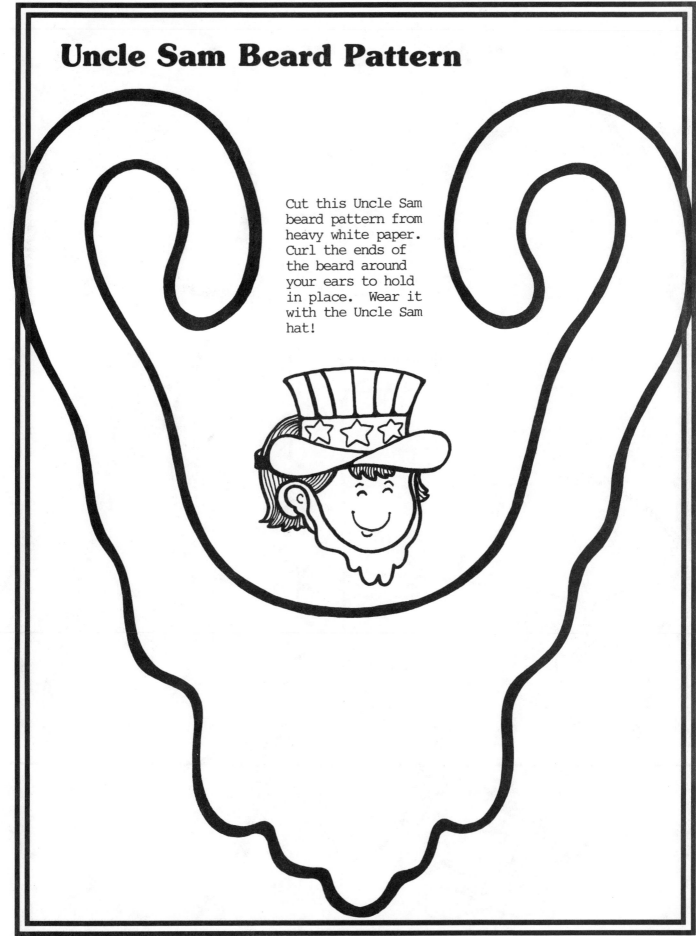

Cut this Uncle Sam beard pattern from heavy white paper. Curl the ends of the beard around your ears to hold in place. Wear it with the Uncle Sam hat!

Uncle Sam Hat

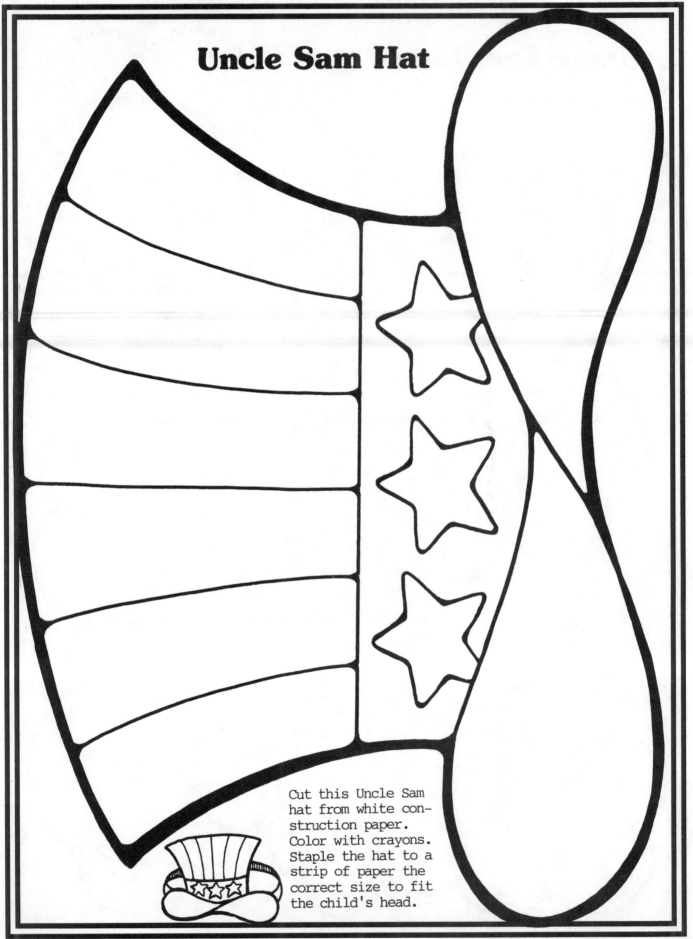

Cut this Uncle Sam hat from white con- struction paper. Color with crayons. Staple the hat to a strip of paper the correct size to fit the child's head.

Stand-Up Shuttle

Cut the space shuttle and cloud from heavy paper. Write your own "out-of-this-world" message across the cloud. Fold along the dotted lines. Glue the shuttle to the cloud and stand on a desk top as a decoration.

Movable Astronaut

Cut this cute astronaut from colored paper and color with crayons or markers.
Use brass fasteners to assemble at the dots.

Teachers might like to award a pattern piece of the astronaut for good behavior or completed assignments. Children can assemble the pieces together
when they have collected all six.

If I Were Stranded On The Moon!......

SUPER STUDENT AWARD

awarded to

_____

for

_____

_____

_____

_____
Date

_____
Teacher

STUDENT OF THE MONTH

AWARDED TO

_____
Name

_____

_____

_____   _____
Teacher   Date

August Activities

AUGUST

August is a summer month.
The temperatures go soaring.
No holidays are in this month,
It may be somewhat boring.

The weather's always very hot
And everyday with sun.
August is a longer month,
Days add to thirty-one.

THE ENDLESS SUMMER VACATION!

This simple exercise will help even reluctant students look forward to the new school year!

Ask them their thoughts on what would happen if school stayed permanently closed and summer took over the entire 12 months of the year. At first, you may hear delightful shouts of joy, but after a few moments of thought, students will begin to conclude that an endless summer might not be as much fun as they thought. Have them write a few paragraphs about their feelings.

WHAT I DIDN'T DO ON MY SUMMER VACATION!

Children will love having this new twist on the old creative writing idea about summer vacations!

Ask them each to think of things they wish they could have done over the summer, such as; a trip to Disneyland or scuba diving lessons. They should also think of things that they are glad they didn't have to do, such as; no homework or shoveling snow!

Have them put their thoughts down on paper and display them on the class board.

ICE CUBE INVENTIONS

During the hottest part of the summer, give your students a project that will really cool them off.

At the close of the day, announce the following assignment: "Tomorrow, you are each to bring an ice cube from home." A brief discussion might follow as how this feat may be accomplished without melting. But, don't give your students too many ideas. You'll be surprised in the morning to find a wide variety of containers, hand-made and commercial.

Students can judge the effectiveness of each container and award prizes to those that provided the best insulated containers. You might also want to recognize those with the greatest imagination and/or the person with the smallest successful container.

What I Didn't Do On My Summer Vacation!

Type the name of your school, address and telephone number in this space. Include your name and room number, also.

Suggestions for a August newsletter:

If your school has not been in session during the summer months, you might like to send your students some reminders and suggestions regarding the first few days of school.

Note the date of the first day and remind them of the time school begins.

Tell the students and parents about some of the fun things you have planned for them for the coming school year.

List the supplies and materials that you expect students to have on hand the first day of school.

Provide a reading list and ask children to read at least one book from the list prior to the start of school.

Describe the award program that you will be implementing in the classroom.

List your classroom rules and homework policy. Emphasize the good behavior and happy attitude you expect from each student.

Express your joy in having them in your classroom. Make sure that you emphasize how exciting and rewarding you expect the new school year to be. With this in mind, each student will look forward with happy anticipation to the first day of school.

August Clip Art

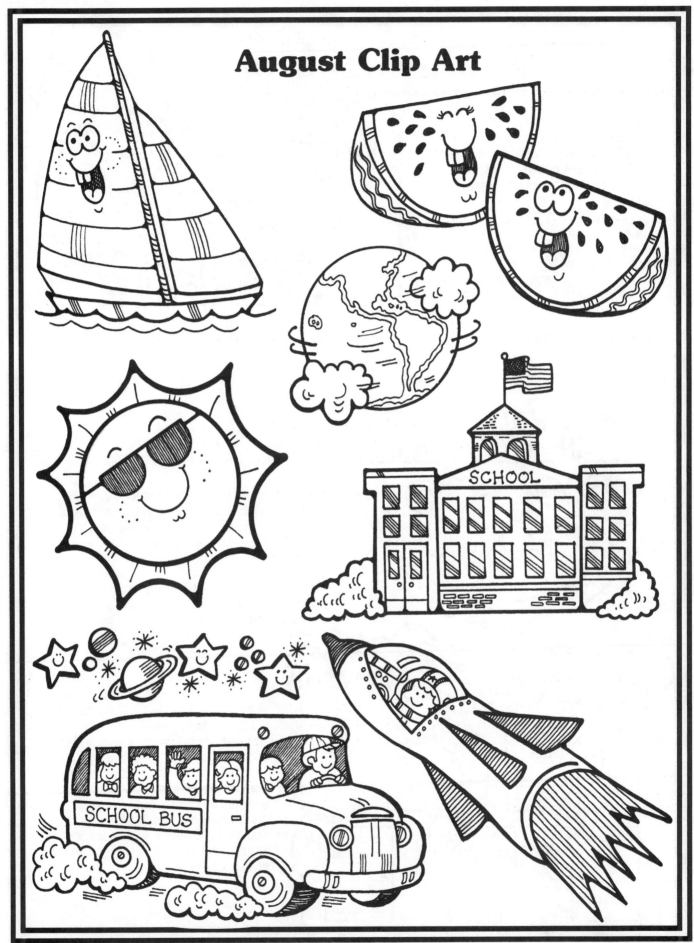

August Bulletin Boards

WATERMELON DAYS!

This delightful bulletin board will help motivate students even through the hottest of summer months!

Display a large, construction paper, slice of watermelon for each student in class. As the children complete required projects or improve behavior, reward them with paper or "real" watermelon seeds. When each student has earned a predetermined number of seeds, celebrate by having a watermelon party!

LOOK WHO'S SPROUTING!

This extra large slice of watermelon is the perfect setting for encouraging students in classroom teamwork. Write each child's name on a black paper watermelon seed with white correction fluid and pin the seeds to the melon slice.

This is also a cute way to welcome students back to school if your school begins in the month of August!

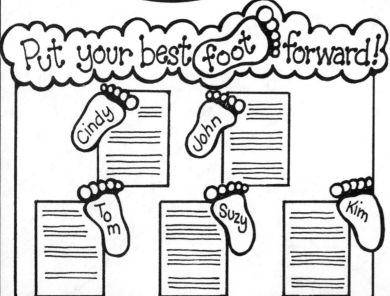

PUT YOUR BEST FOOT FORWARD!

Display good work papers with this effective but easy bulletin board idea. Cut several footprints from colored paper and post them next to each good work paper. Students could also earn stickers or stars and attach them to their footprint!

MY WATERMELON BOOK

Footsteps

Welcome your class to the first day of school with one or more of these "footprint" displays!

Write each student's name on a footprint pattern made from colored construction paper. Pin them in a walking sequence across the classroom door or bulletin board. Use the title, "Step Right Up to Learning!" Or, "Step In For A Great Year!"

Display good work papers along with glittered footprints for a "Fancy Footwork" display!

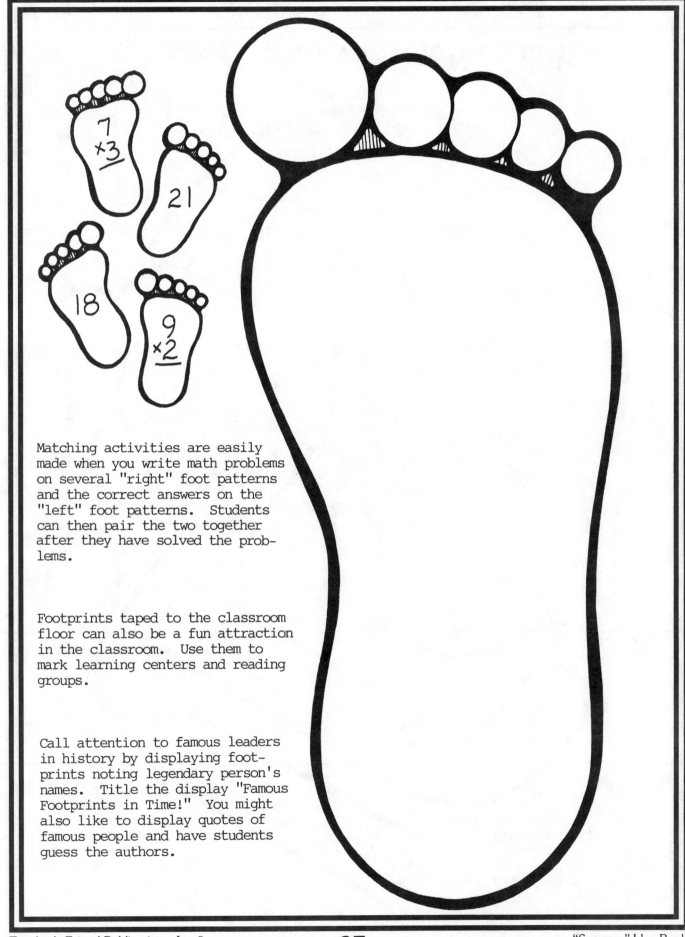

Matching activities are easily
made when you write math problems
on several "right" foot patterns
and the correct answers on the
"left" foot patterns. Students
can then pair the two together
after they have solved the problems.

Footprints taped to the classroom
floor can also be a fun attraction
in the classroom. Use them to
mark learning centers and reading
groups.

Call attention to famous leaders
in history by displaying footprints noting legendary person's
names. Title the display "Famous
Footprints in Time!" You might
also like to display quotes of
famous people and have students
guess the authors.

August Sunglasses and Visor

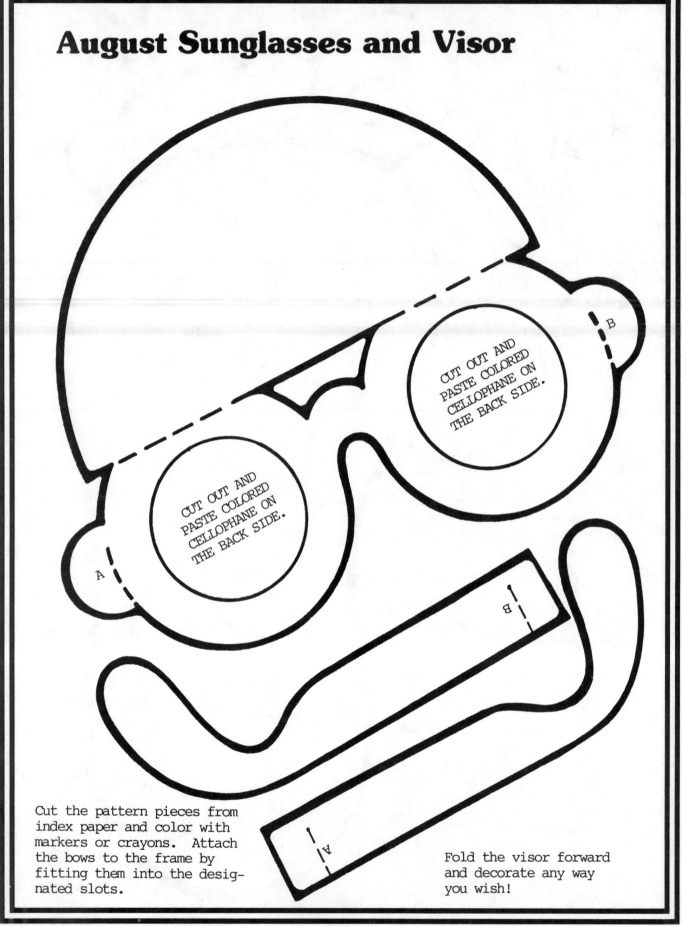

CUT OUT AND PASTE COLORED CELLOPHANE ON THE BACK SIDE.

CUT OUT AND PASTE COLORED CELLOPHANE ON THE BACK SIDE.

Cut the pattern pieces from index paper and color with markers or crayons. Attach the bows to the frame by fitting them into the designated slots.

Fold the visor forward and decorate any way you wish!

Stand-Up Stars

Cut the stars and pencil character from heavy paper. Write your own name or message across the stars. Fan fold along the dotted lines. Glue the pencil to the first star and stand on a desk top as a name tag or back to school decoration.

CLEAN UP GAMEBOARD

START

1. 2. 3. 4. 5. 6. 7. 8. 9. 10. 11. 12. 13. 14. 15.

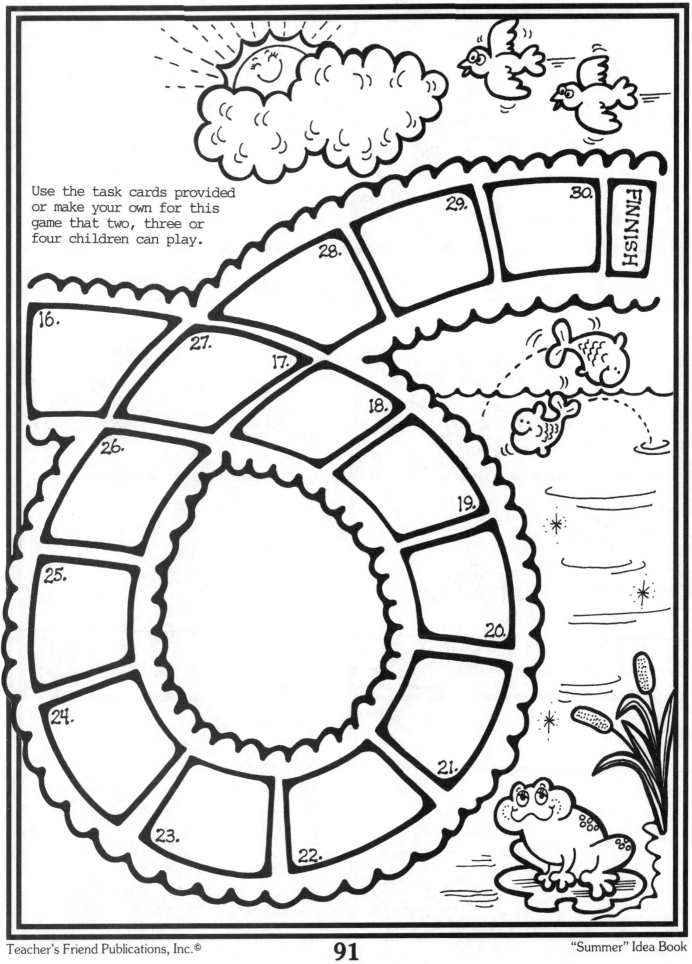

Use the task cards provided
or make your own for this
game that two, three or
four children can play.

FINNISH

16.
27.
17.
18.
19.
20.
21.
22.
23.
24.
25.
26.
28.
29.
30.

YOU PLANTED A TREE TO
CELEBRATE ARBOR DAY!

MOVE AHEAD 1 SPACE

YOU ORGANIZE A NEIGHBOR-
HOOD CLEAN-UP CAMPAIGN!

MOVE AHEAD 2 SPACES

YOU CONTRIBUTE TO AN ENVIRON-
MENTAL GROUP THAT HELPS PASS
LAWS TO CONTROL POLLUTERS!

MOVE AHEAD 3 SPACES

YOU HELPED CLEAN UP GRAFFITI
AT YOUR NEIGHBORHOOD SCHOOL!

TAKE ANOTHER TURN

YOU SAVED WATER BY NOT
HOSING OFF YOUR WALKWAYS
OR DRIVEWAY!

GO AHEAD 1 SPACE

YOU RECYCLED ALL OF YOUR
PLASTIC, GLASS AND PAPER!

MOVE AHEAD 3 SPACES

YOU JOINED A CAR POOL!

MOVE AHEAD 2 SPACES

YOU CONSERVE ENERGY BY USING
APPLIANCES ONLY IN THE EVEN-
ING AND TURNING OFF LIGHTS
WHEN NOT IN USE!

TAKE ANOTHER TURN

YOU FAIL TO RECYCLE
YOUR TRASH!

GO BACK 3 SPACES

YOU LITTERED!

GO BACK 3 SPACES

YOU BURN LEAVES IN YOUR
BACK YARD INSTEAD OF
RECYCLING THEM IN YOUR
GARDEN!

GO BACK 1 SPACE

YOU POURED INSECTICIDE
DOWN THE DRAIN!

LOSE A TURN

YOU WROTE GRAFFITI ON A
NEIGHBORHOOD WALL!!!

LOSE A TURN

YOU WASTED WATER BY
OVERWATERING YOUR LAWN!

GO BACK 2 SPACES

YOU WASTE GASOLINE BY ALWAYS
USING YOUR CAR INSTEAD OF
PUBLIC TRANSPORTATION!

GO BACK 1 SPACE

YOU WASTE ELECTRICITY AND
POWER BY USING APPLIANCES
DURING PEAK HOURS.

GO BACK 2 SPACES

Ecology Mobile

Each child can make his or her own Ecology Mobile by cutting these pattern pieces from colored construction paper. (They may want to mount the finished pieces on posterboard for added durability.)

TAKE CARE OF OUR EARTH

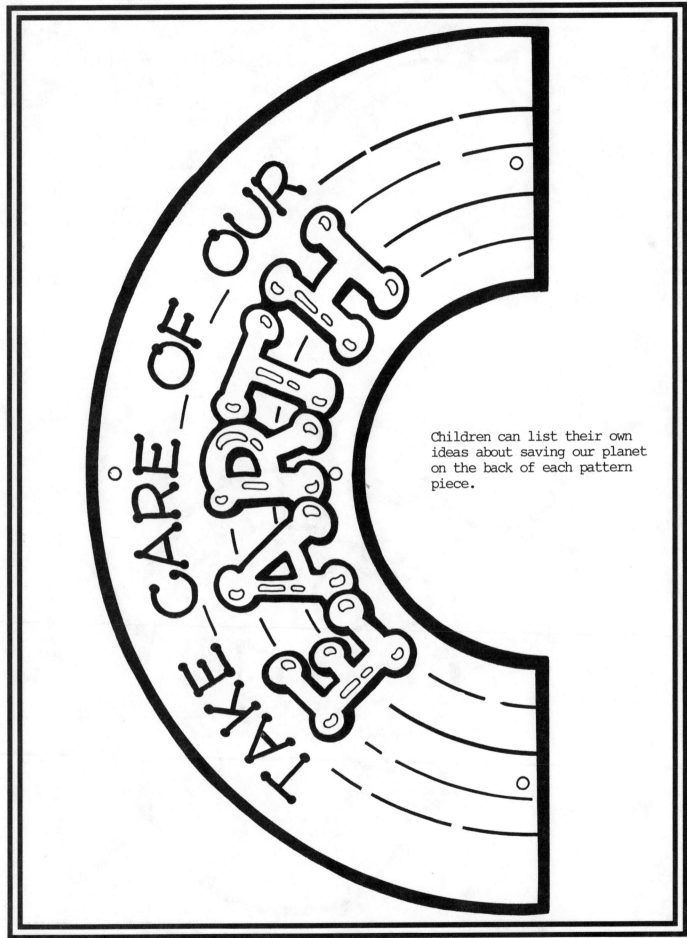

Children can list their own ideas about saving our planet on the back of each pattern piece.

Ecology **Button**

Member of the

ECOLOGY CLUB

BASEBALL

Baseball Activities

BASEBALL

A baseball game is so much fun!
Hit the ball and then you run.
First base, second and on to third,
The ball you hit flies like a bird.

As you quickly round the bases,
People watch with anxious faces.
People watching smile and shout,
"Run to home before you're out!"

Slide into home, you can, you must,
Never mind the dirt and dust.
"You made it!" People cheer so loud!
The team is glad and aren't you proud!

Baseball Bingo

This game offers an exciting way to introduce students to baseball vocabulary words. Give each child a copy of the bingo words listed below or write the words on the chalkboard. Ask students to write any 24 words on his or her bingo cards. Use the same directions you might use for regular bingo.

(Students might like to use some of these words in a creative writing assignment.)

BASEBALL	CENTER FIELD	DOUBLE	KNUCKLE BALL
BAT	LEFT FIELD	TRIPLE	CURVE BALL
MITT	COACH	HOME RUN	POP FLY
PITCHER	BATTER	OUT	BUNT
CATCHER	STRIKE	STEAL	WALK
1st BASE	BALL	SLIDE	CROWD
2nd BASE	RUNS	SAFE	FANS
3rd BASE	INNINGS	HOME	STADIUM
SHORTSTOP	SCORE	FAST BALL	GAME
RIGHT FIELD	SINGLE	SLOW BALL	SERIES

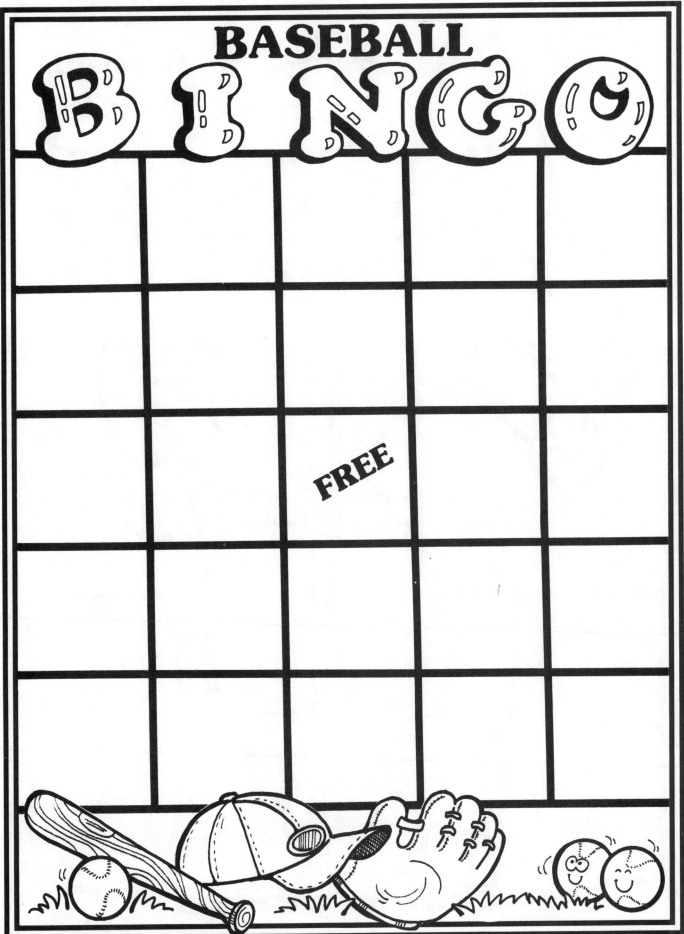

BASEBALL BINGO

FREE

Teacher's Friend Publications, Inc.©

"Summer" Idea Book

Baseball Character

Cut this cute baseball character from index paper. Color, cut out and fold. Attach the baseball bat to his right hand and stand on a table for a decoration.

Matching Baseballs and Mitts

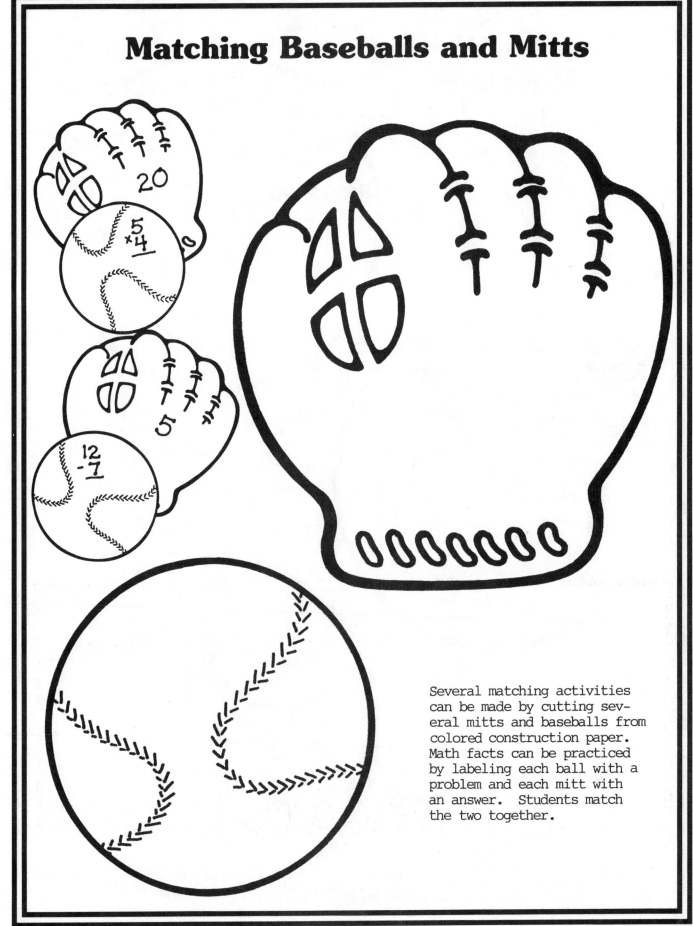

Several matching activities can be made by cutting several mitts and baseballs from colored construction paper. Math facts can be practiced by labeling each ball with a problem and each mitt with an answer. Students match the two together.

Creative Writing
Baseballs

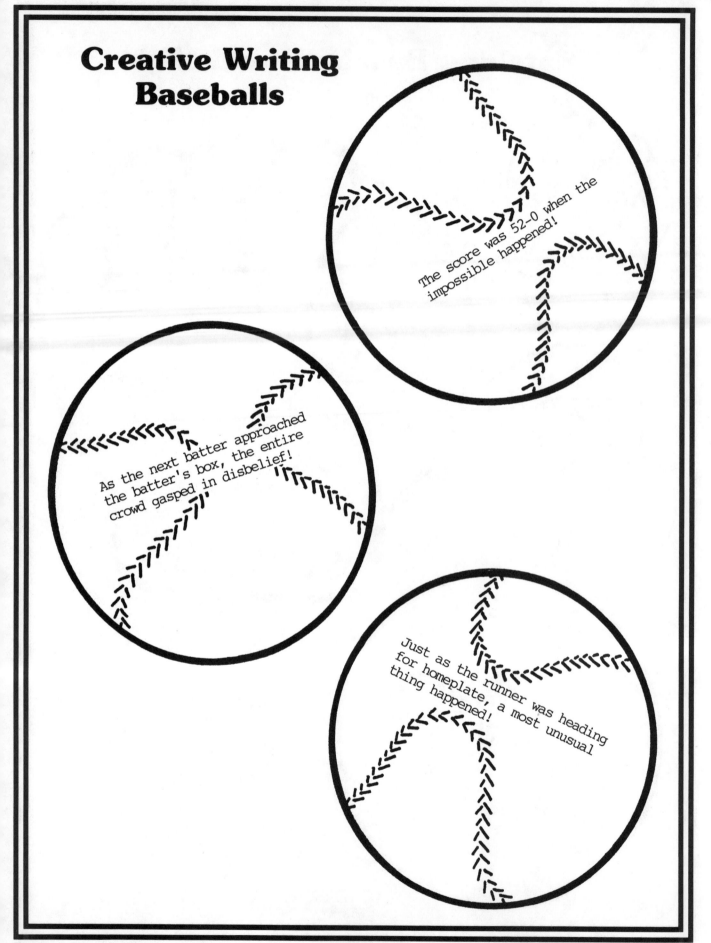

The score was 52-0 when the impossible happened!

As the next batter approached the batter's box, the entire crowd gasped in disbelief!

Just as the runner was heading for homeplate, a most unusual thing happened!

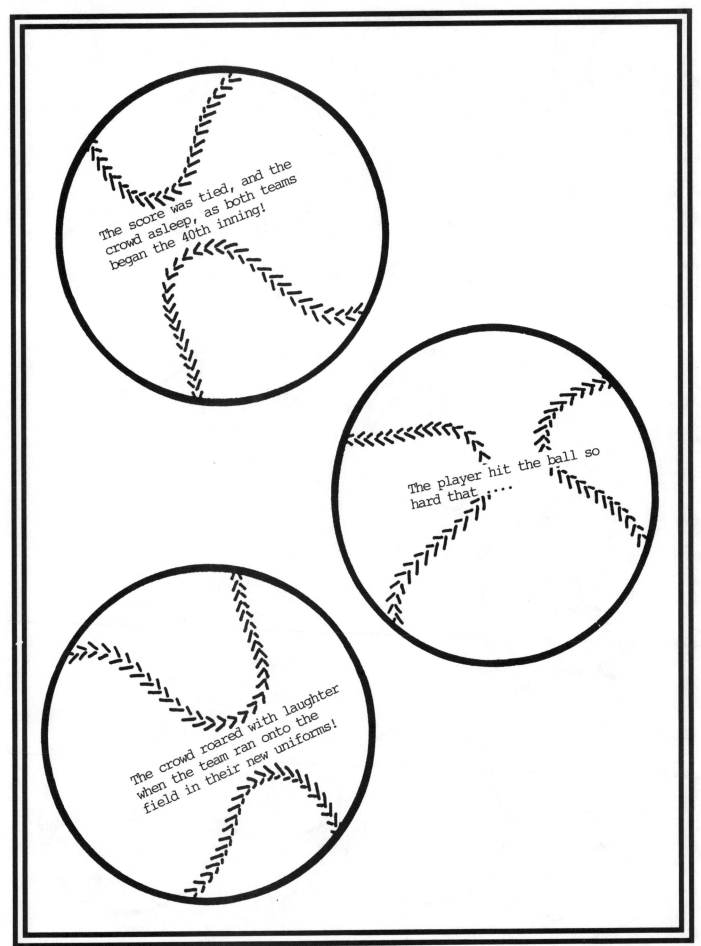

The score was tied, and the crowd asleep, as both teams began the 40th inning!

The player hit the ball so hard that....

The crowd roared with laughter when the team ran onto the field in their new uniforms!

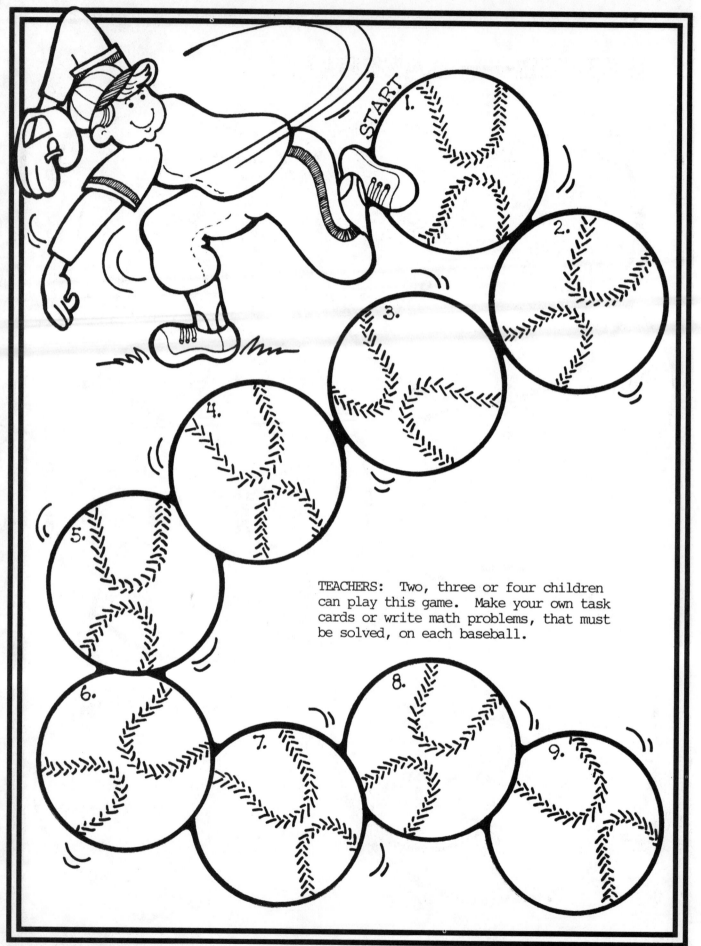

START

1.

2.

3.

4.

5.

TEACHERS: Two, three or four children can play this game. Make your own task cards or write math problems, that must be solved, on each baseball.

6.

7.

8.

9.

BATTER-UP BASEBALL!

Baseball Bulletin Boards

GRAND SLAM STORIES!

Children will love writing creative sport stories using these mitt and baseball booklets. Arrange the booklets on the class board with the title, "Grand Slam Stories!"

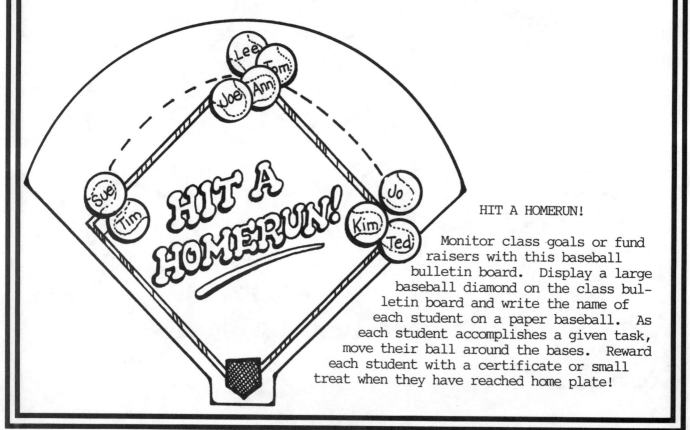

HIT A HOMERUN!

Monitor class goals or fund raisers with this baseball bulletin board. Display a large baseball diamond on the class bulletin board and write the name of each student on a paper baseball. As each student accomplishes a given task, move their ball around the bases. Reward each student with a certificate or small treat when they have reached home plate!

Catcher's Mitt Booklet

Baseball Booklet